The [barcode] of FORMULA 1 to the rhythm of fast lap

Keys to review its history and evolution and enjoy the best motorsport competition to the fullest

Formula 1 is the obsession to be the fastest on the asphalt. It is the passion for that split second that separates success from failure. But what is it that we are so passionate about this sport that it can be summed up in a single word: speed?

Formula 1 is what you don't see before the green light: technology to polish that piece that allows you to start a few thousandths from the stopwatch; develop the most powerful engine to make the car fly on the track or control the wind to convert it into a few extra kilometers per hour through aerodynamics. Formula 1 is ingenuity and effort to get the fastest beast on the grid.

But Formula 1 is also what you see on the asphalt. Battles on the track on the border between life and death, overtaking outside the line at more than 300 km / h, devouring the pianos to the extreme assuming the risk of an accident or leaving the track ...

Formula 1 is also prestige, responsibility, brands risking their image and the honor of creating the most powerful vehicle on the face of the Earth.

But above all, Formula 1 is its history. I would not be covered with that halo of heroism without those who through control of time and speed became heroes on the asphalt.

The Fangio revolution, the Lotus years, Ferrari's eternal struggle through time, the rise of Williams, the rivalry between Ayrton Senna and Alain Prost, the legend of Kaiser Michael Schumacher, the best years of McLaren, Alonso and Renault , the dominance of Red Bull and Vettel, the super champion Hamilton and the hybrid era of Mercedes ...

Formula 1 would not be what it is without the glory of the past years poured into each of the great prizes, which bring memories of yesterday to our present. You don't enjoy this sport so much without knowing its route, its history, the greatness that one day was and will continue to be and that comes back to our minds every time the engines roar.

That is the objective of this book: a simple walk through its history so that every new Formula 1 fan can enjoy the origins and years that mythologized this sport, so that they feel the weight of history, thus adding one more dose of passion for the best motorsport championship today. It is also a walk for those who enjoyed their past and want to remember and bask in the blessed nostalgia for those races that will never return.

Because Formula 1 continually changes, but the passion always remains. I hope you enjoy this journey through time and that these keys make you know, remember and enjoy even more the passion of this sport.

Let the engines start!

Silverstone, 1950: the beginning of it all

On May 13, 1950, in Great Britain, at the Silverstone circuit, the single-seaters began to roll, beginning a championship that would grow in importance until creating the passion that Formula 1 is today for all its fans.

Previously, the European Drivers' Championship had already been established in 1931, unifying several of the most important grands prix that previously acted as independent events. However, after six editions, the irruption of World War II ended up making the championship disappear.

Motoresapleno.com.ar

After the war, the AIACR (Association Internationale des Automobile Clubs Reconnus), was reorganized giving rise to the FIA (International Automobile Federation), establishing the rules of a new Formula 1: 4.5-liter atmospheric or supercharged 1 ,5 liters. For 1950, the first Drivers' World Championship was organized, bringing together six of the most important grands prix.

In this first edition the calendar would consist of the great prizes of Great Britain (Silverstone), Monaco (Monte Carlo), Switzerland (Bremgarten), Belgium (Spa), France (Reims-Gueux) and Italy (Monza). Due to its impact, the Indianapolis 500 would also be included as a scoring event. Only the first five drivers scored (counting only their best four races) plus an additional point for the fastest lap, and if two drivers had to share the same vehicle, the points were shared.

The Mercedes-Benz or Auto Union, German vehicles that had dominated before the war, were missed at the opening of the championship.

However, everything was ready and the first edition of the Formula 1 Drivers' World Championship began.

Giuseppe Farina, the first champion

Italian Giuseppe Farina would be the first driver to cross the finish line in a world championship race by taking first place at Silverstone. This would make him the first driver to achieve a victory in this sport.

This victory, together with that of Switzerland and Italy, would also lead him at 44 to win the championship title, extending his feat to become the first champion of a Formula 1 world competition.

He would do it aboard the Alfa Romeo 158, a voiturette that was invincible as this team achieved the six championship victories on European soil.

Pinterest.co.uk

The main rival of Nino Farina for the championship was the Argentine Juan Manuel Fangio, who only managed to lead by three points. The third classified was the Italian Luigi Fagioli, being the three Alfa Romeo drivers, thus demonstrating the power of this team in this first edition of the championship.

Leonardasf1.narod.ru

Monaco, 1950, the debut of a historical: Ferrari

It wasn't until the second race of the World Drivers' Championship that Scuderia Ferrari made an appearance in the competition. Although he could not attend the first appointment at Silverstone, the prestigious Italian team debuted on May 21 in Monaco. Since then, she would become the only one today to participate in all editions of the championship.

The best positioned driver for Ferrari in this first season was Alberto Ascari, finishing sixth in the final standings with 11 points. Ascari achieved second place in Monaco and Monza (in the latter with Dorino Serafini). Luigi Villoresi, Raymond Sommer, Dorino Serafini and Peter Whitehead were also on its squad.

Ferrari participated in this edition with the 125, 275 and 375 models.

1951: Fangio's revenge

The second season of the World Championship began as the first ended, with Alfa Romeo dominating its rivals. However, throughout the championship, Ferrari was improving its development while Alfa remained stagnant, finding a dangerous rival in the Scuderia. In fact, Ferrari had already shown its ability to compete in the non-scoring grand prix before the start of the championship.

At the British Grand Prix, Alfa Romeo showed its weakness when it comes to fuel efficiency, having to make two pit stops, which allowed the Ferrari of Argentine José Froilán González to win.
Alfa Romeo was defeated for the first time on European soil and Ferrari achieved its first victory in the championship.

Parabrisas.perfil.com

After the victory of José Froilán González, the two consecutive Ascari in Germany and Italy would come, leaving Fangio only two points ahead for the last race of the season: Spain. Ascari got the pole for the last grand prix, however a wrong choice of tires made Fangio win the race and therefore the championship at 40 years old, becoming the second champion of the competition and obtaining his little personal revenge against his partner Farina, who would be fourth.

Es.wikipedia.org

Ferrari and Ascari fill Alfa Romeo void

The main surprise in the third edition of the championship was the absence of Alfa Romeo, a team that had achieved victory in the first two editions. The Italian government refused to finance a new car and this led to the withdrawal of the team.

This endangered the competitiveness of the championship, as Ferrari was left without competition and with relative superiority. To avoid this, the FIA adopted the rules of Formula 2, forcing Ferrari to regulate its superior 4.5-liter engine. By adopting cheaper regulation, more teams were also expected to join.

Following the withdrawal of Alfa Romeo, Farina accepted Ferrari's offer, but had to do so under the shadow of Ascari. For his part, an accident by Fangio in a non-scoring event at Monza prevented him from participating in the championship.

Thus the things and in spite of the attempts of the FIA to obtain the equality, Ferrari dominated and through Ascari it gained six of the seven tests in European territory. He only did not get the victory in Switzerland and because he did not participate as he was preparing the 500 Miles. Absolute dominance of Ascari, who was proclaimed champion at 34, and first Ferrari title.

En.wikipedia.org

The following year, also under Formula 2 regulations, Ferrari would once again be the undisputed leader. Ascari won the first three races of the championship (not counting the 500 Miles) bringing the number of consecutive victories to 9, and would win two more to claim his second world title.

His winning streak would only be interrupted by Mike Hawthorn, also for Ferrari. The Englishman had earned a place in the team after his good work in the previous season.

Motorclasic.ro

Farina would manage to win the German Grand Prix to be third in the championship, and Fangio would emerge victorious from Italy, aboard the Maserati, to get the runner-up and avoid the full of triumphs for Ferrari.

This season would be characterized as the first to include a race on South American soil, the Argentine Grand Prix in Buenos Aires. However, she would be remembered for the tragedy in which 9 people died after an accident.

F1-web.com.ar

Motor.es

1954: The return of Fangio

If anyone could end the hegemony of Ferrari, that was Juan Manuel Fangio. Thus, the Argentine achieved victory in the opening race of the 1954 season on his own land. In Belgium he would win the victory again with Maserati, hitting the table.

Then, Fangio went on to drive for Mercedes Benz, which made its debut in France and did so in a spectacular way, with a great advantage over its rivals and getting a double thanks to Fangio and Karl Kling. However, at Silverstone the Mercedes accused the aerodynamics and gave Ferrari a break, which returned the double on British soil.

Mercedes learned from mistakes and redesigned the chassis in a show of German efficiency, leading to Fangio winning the next three races (Germany, Switzerland and Italy) and leading the Argentine to his second world title.

Weltmeister 1954 auf Mercedes-Benz Juan Manuel Fangio

Aufnahme: Pfeil   Mercedes-Benz Fotodienst (54)

Catawiki.com

Hawthorn closed the season with an insufficient victory at Monza for Ferrari, which had found a formidable rival in Mercedes, despite the fact that its drivers José Froilán González had secured the runner-up and Hawthorn third place.

Eufixe.com

1955: The Le Mans disaster

In 1955 a rule change extended to five the maximum races of the championship in which a pilot could score, thus accounting for his five best performances of the eleven possible after the return from Monaco and Holland.

However, a tragedy changed the course of the competition: the Le Mans disaster. On June 11 at the Circuit de la Sarthe, during the legendary 24 Hours of Le Mans race, an accident killed the driver Pierre Levegh and 83 spectators, being considered the worst tragedy in motorsports.

Although the race was not suspended (and Mike Hawthorn would eventually win it), the races in France, Germany, Spain and Switzerland were suspended, altering the calendar of the Formula 1 World Championship.

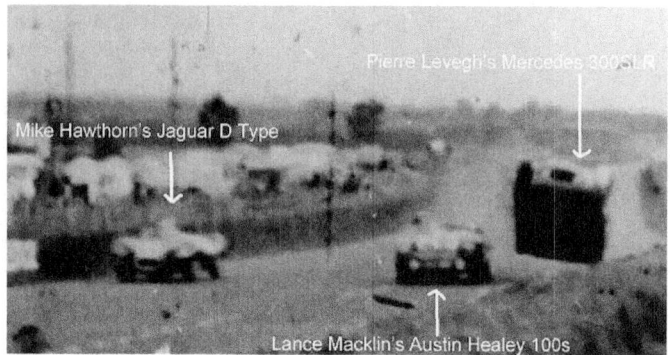
Autoblog.com.ar

These changes would not alter the trend of the competition, in which Fangio was once again the most prominent along with Mercedes, winning 5 of the 7 races held and comfortably obtaining his third world title (second in a row), thus expanding his legend.

Pinterest.es

Cochesclasicosdehoy.com

The versatility of Fangio and his legend

After the withdrawal of Mercedes after the disaster at Le Mans, Ferrari did not miss the option of returning to dominate the orbit of Formula 1: sign Fangio. The Argentine complied from the beginning by winning the first race, although he had to do it with his teammate Luigi Musso's car after a breakdown in his own.

However, things for Fangio weren't easy at all. Stirling Moss, who would eventually be remembered as the best performing driver ever to win a championship title, showed remarkable consistency by winning two races with Maserati. Both BRM and Vanwall also performed well in the race.

However, the biggest threat to Fangio was his teammate Peter Collins, who was only 8 points ahead of the last race of the championship: Monza. If Fangio did not score and Collins managed to win, in addition to the fastest lap, the title would go to the British.

Already in the race, Fangio had a breakdown in his vehicle, so he suggested using that of his partner Luigi Musso as the only alternative to continue. The Italian refused, but then it was Collins himself, in a remarkable act of sportsmanship and respect within the team, who gave his car to Fangio, who would finish second in the race adding his fourth world title (third in a row), this time with Ferrari, thus demonstrating its versatility.

Accidentesmortalef1.blogspot.com

In 1957, Fangio changed teams again, this time joining Maserati. This turned out to be a wise decision, as Ferrari diminished its performance and was unable to achieve victory in any of the grand prixes.

The sporting decline joined the personal tragedy after the death of two of its drivers out of competition: the Italian Eugenio Castelloti and Alfonso de Portago, the first Spanish driver who had managed to drive for Ferrari.

Autobild.es

This season, Fangio found his main competitor in Stirling Moss, who after signing for Vanwall, managed to win three races to return to runner-up behind Fangio, who won four victories. The Argentine thus achieved his fifth world title (once again with a different car), and fourth in a row.

At the end of the season, Fangio announced his retirement with five world titles, having forged a legend in Formula 1. In the same way, Maserati also abandoned due to its financial situation.

Subdivx.com

1958: The World Constructors' Championship and the most tragic season

In 1958, the FIA created the World Constructors' Championship for the first time. The brands thus acquired another incentive to compete by adding professional prestige beyond trying to lead one of their pilots to the title.

However, despite this initiative, the 1958 season would be remembered for being the most tragic in Formula 1 when four drivers died in four different races.

Luigi Musso, Ferrari driver, would lose his life at the French Grand Prix (Reims). His partner Peter Collins would do it in Germany (Nürburgring). Stuart Lewins-Evans, a Vanwall driver, would suffer an accident in Morocco and American Pat O'Connor would die in Indianapolis.

In the sports part, Mike Hawthorn would take advantage of the first season of the post Fangio era to win the title driving the Ferrari 143 2.4 V6. After getting the title, he would retire from the championship although, paradoxically, he would end up dying months later in a traffic accident.

Magazine.ferrari.com

Despite the victory of the Ferrari driver, the first constructors' title would go to Vanwall, thanks to the performances of Stirling Moss (runner-up once again), Tony Brooks and the late Stuart Lewis-Evans, who knew how to take advantage of the Vanwall's performance 254 2.5 L4 to get 6 victories throughout the championship.

Es.wikipedia.org

The abandonment of the front engines

In 1959, most of the vehicles abandoned the front engine, changing it for one in the central position (except for Ferrari, which would take time to move its engine until 1961). In this new change, Cooper surprised with his 2.5-liter rear Coventry Climax engine, which, driven by Jack Brabham, Stirling Moss and Bruce McLaren, would end up taking the constructors' title by achieving victory in five races.

Of their drivers, both Brabham and Moss had options in the last race in the United States to be named champions, along with Tony Brooks of Ferrari. Moss had to retire due to technical problems, once again on the verge of success.

Brabham, for his part, ran out of gas, being forced to push his car... to cross the finish line and become world champion.

Es.wikipedia.org

The following year, 1960, was the last of the 2.5-liter engines. The trend would be continuous from the previous year, with no changes beyond eliminating the point per fast lap and expanding the scoring positions to six.

Cooper would dominate even more comfortably than the previous season, winning his second consecutive constructors' title, and with victory again for Jack Brabham, who would add his second championship.

Pinterest.co.uk

This season the upgrade of rear-engined teams was confirmed, with Lotus, BRM and Porsche prevailing over front-engined cars.

It was also the last year that the Indianapolis 500 was eligible for the Formula 1 championship.

Fast-mag.com

1.5 liter engines

1961 was the first year of the 1.5-liter engines, a change to which Ferrari, together with the adoption of the rear engine, adapted more quickly, judging by the absolute dominance in the competition.

The Italian team won five of the eight races, and only Lotus was able to beat them. Ferrari thus managed to return to the top by winning the constructors' title and among its drivers, Phil Hill would be the first American to achieve a world title.

Diezcilindros.wordpress.com

In the French Grand Prix, the pilot Giancarlo Baghetti would achieve the feat of winning a race with a private vehicle, made by Ferrari. This is somewhat more impressive considering that it was his debut in the competition.

Database.motorsportmagazine.com

Nor would he be spared this season of tragedy when, at Monza, Wolfgang von Trips collided with Jim Clark, blowing the German's car through the air, killing him and 14 fans.

Alchetron.com

The British rise

Ferrari's victory in 1960 would be a fleeting success, as in 1961 the team was overwhelmed by the push of the British teams. Despite the good start to the season, the Italian team suffered a strike in the middle of the championship that forced them not to participate in the last two Grand Prix.

Ferrari's void was quickly filled by BRM (British Racing Motors), who won both the constructors 'and drivers' titles, which would go to Graham Hill. The British driver would get four victories that would lead him to win the championship.

BRM's biggest rival was Lotus, which at the hands of Jim Clark, surprised by its monocoque design, being the first Formula 1 manufactured in a single piece.

For its part, the Porsche team would achieve its first (and only) victory in a grand prix at the hands of the American Dan Gurney in France (Rouen).

Also noteworthy is the role of Jack Brabham, who managed to score points this time with his own team.

As for Stirling Moss, he had signed for Ferrari but an accident prior to the championship prevented him from contesting the season, and in fact he would no longer compete in a Formula 1 Grand Prix. The "champion without a crown", one of the drivers with the best results without ever winning the world title.

Elotroladodelascarreras.blog

In 1963 it would be a British team that would get the constructors' title. This time it would be Lotus, which had already surprised by its monocoque design, and now it was also with its performance. The Lotus-Climax team would also lead the British driver Jim Clark to win the championship, setting the record of winning seven races in the same season.

Hockenheim-historic.de

The 1964 season featured a very close match between Jim Clark, Graham Hill and John Surtees. The three pilots, British, thus showed the rise of the United Kingdom in the competition. In the last race, Hill collided with Lorenzo Bandini's Ferrari while Clark suffered an oil leak that forced him to stop. Thus, Surtees ended up becoming the world champion.

Amcn.com.au

John Surtees was proclaimed champion aboard a Ferrari, which also achieved the constructors' title, rising again to the top. Surtees got the title thanks to the fact that, with team orders, his teammate Bandini let him pass on the last lap.

Ar.pinterest.com

In 1965 the Lotus-Clark duo returned to achieve success. The Lotus team won its second constructors 'title, while Jim Clark also won his second (and last) drivers' title.

Clark got the victory in six of the first seven races, he only needed to win in Monaco, which he did not appear because he was preparing the Indianapolis 500, which by the way he also managed to win.

Macsmotorcitygarage.com

1965 would also be remembered as the year in which Honda would get its first victory (after having debuted the previous year), and it would do so in Mexico with Richie Ginther.

Motorpasion.com

1966: 3-liter engines

In 1966 the engine capacity was doubled to 3 liters. In addition, a new rule was established that it was necessary to complete at least 90% of the race to score points, and the maximum mileage of these was reduced from 500 to 400 kilometers.

The changes allowed Australian Jack Brabham to win the drivers 'world title again for the second time, and his team, Brabham-Repco, to win the constructors' title.

Brabham won four consecutive races leading to the title. John Surtees, who was runner-up, won the second race of the season with Ferrari, and also the last, but with Cooper-Maserati.

The following year, in 1967 Brabham-Repco would once again win the constructors' title, obtaining its second and last title.

En.wikipedia.org

However, the drivers' title went to New Zealander Denny Hulme, Jack Brabham's teammate, although he would end up being runner-up. The funny thing about Hulme is that he would be the first driver to be proclaimed champion without having achieved any pole. Jim Clark, despite achieving four victories with Lotus, could only finish third.

This season, at the Dutch Grand Prix, Lotus used one of the most victorious engines in history, the Ford Cosworth DFV.

Pinterest.es

For his part, Mexican Pedro Rodríguez de la Vega would get Cooper's last victory in the South African Grand Prix.

Already in the following season, in 1968, Lotus asserted its commitment to the Ford Cosworth engine and returned to the top with its third manufacturer's title. He would do so by leading Britain's Graham Hill to win the drivers' championship after winning three races, the same as his top competitor Jackie Stewart.

Cochesclasicosdehoy.com

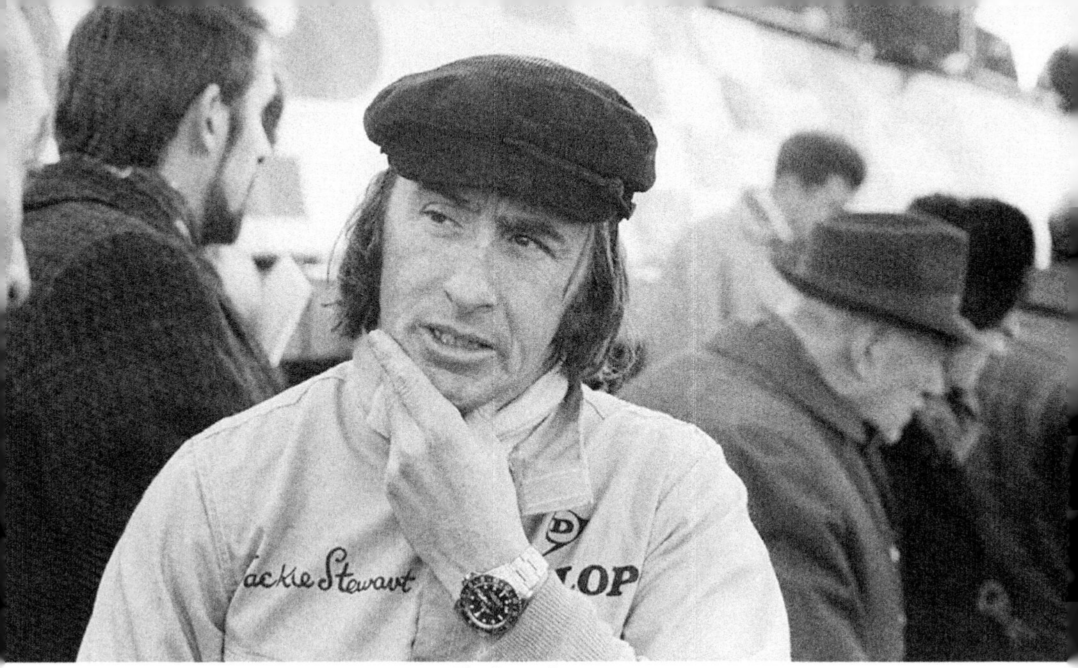

Eluniversal.com.mx

The glory of Jackie Stewart and the aerodynamic changes

In 1969, the Matra brand decided to focus exclusively on the Matra International team, boosting the team in competitiveness to the point of claiming the constructors 'title, leading Jackie Stewart to win his first drivers' championship.

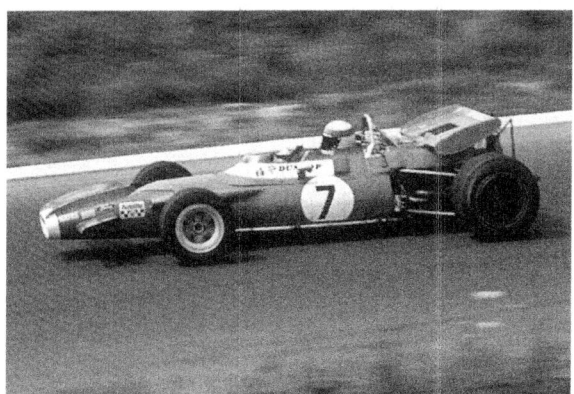

Es.wikipedia.org

Matra's achievement is remarkable since he had started to compete the previous season, and once the competition had already started. It marks the first victory for a French team and a vehicle with a chassis made in France. For more glory, Stewart nearly doubled second-placed Jacky Ickx's Brabham in points.

This season the use of ailerons was prohibited due to their danger, although they would end up being allowed again, but with weight and size restrictions and as long as they were attached to the chassis and not to the suspensions.

There is also a special attraction for 4x4 traction, although only one car with traction would score points and in fact most drivers hated driving this type of vehicle. Ford further discovered that its engine was efficient when power was transmitted to the rear wheels.

Other technical changes that became important were the use of wide wheels and the use of the ground effect in order to achieve more grip.

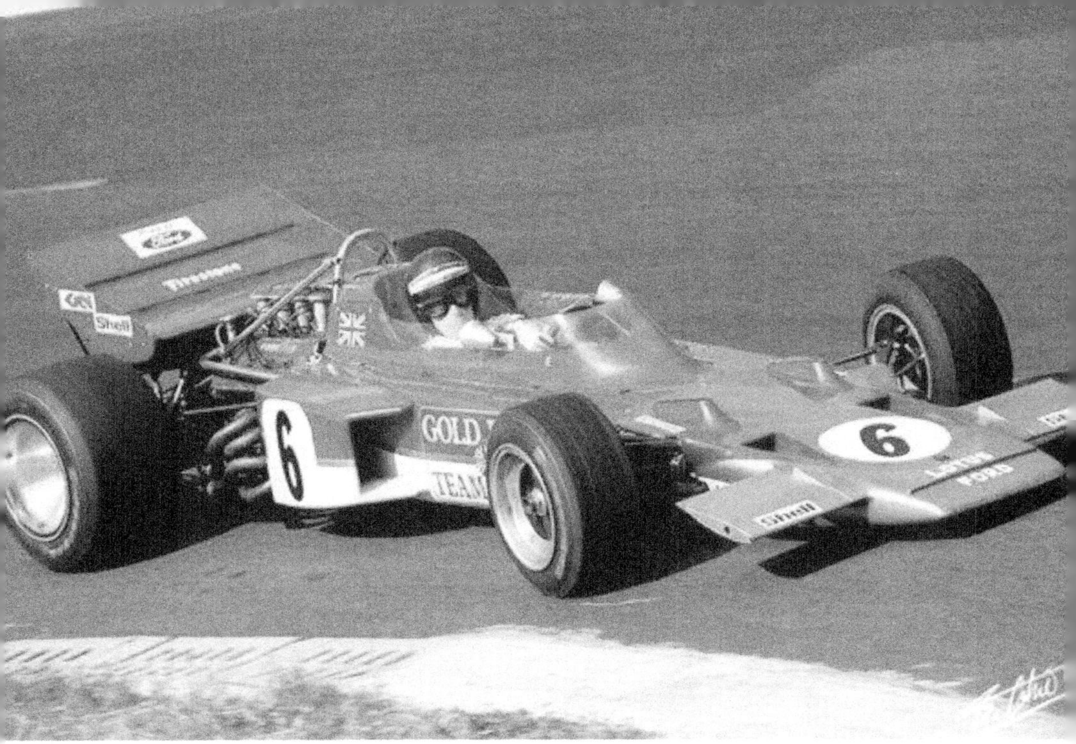

Ar.pinterest.com

The posthumous title of Jochen Rindt

In 1970, Lotus once again demonstrated its constant competitiveness and once again won the constructors' title by winning 6 of the 13 races. He did it thanks to the Austrian pilot Jochen Rindt, who achieved victory in five grands prix that would earn him the drivers' title. He would achieve it, sadly, posthumously when he died in the Italian Grand Prix practice before finishing the championship that he would end up winning, this being the only case with these characteristics throughout the history of the competition.

Es.wikipedia.org

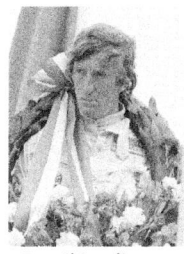

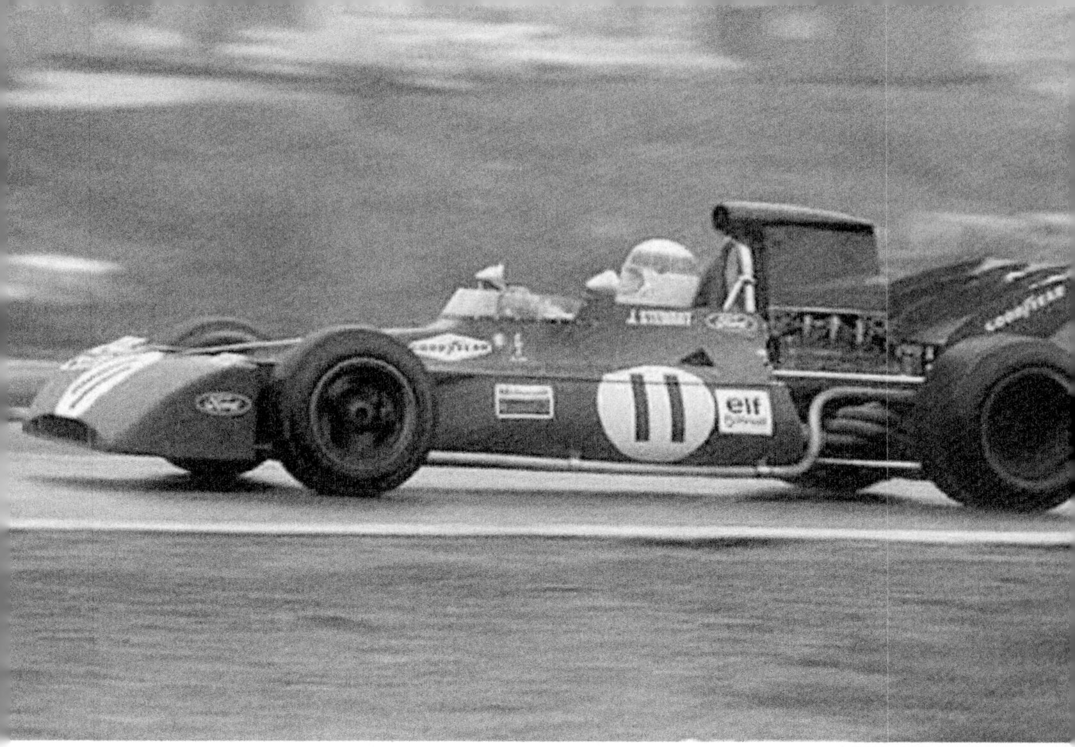

Snaplap.net

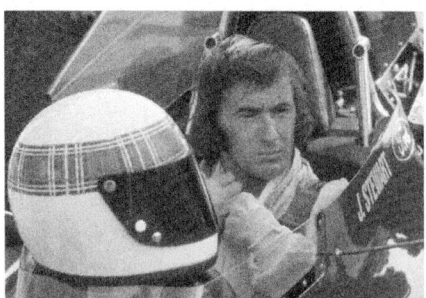

Jackie Stewart adds and goes

In 1971, Jackie Stewart would be proclaimed champion again, this time aboard a Tyrrell team car, the first and only time that he would manage to lift the constructors' title. Stewart also beat with relative ease, leading by 29 points to his immediate pursuer, the Swede Ronnie Peterson who was driving for March.

Sportskeeda.com

Cochesclasicosdehoy.com

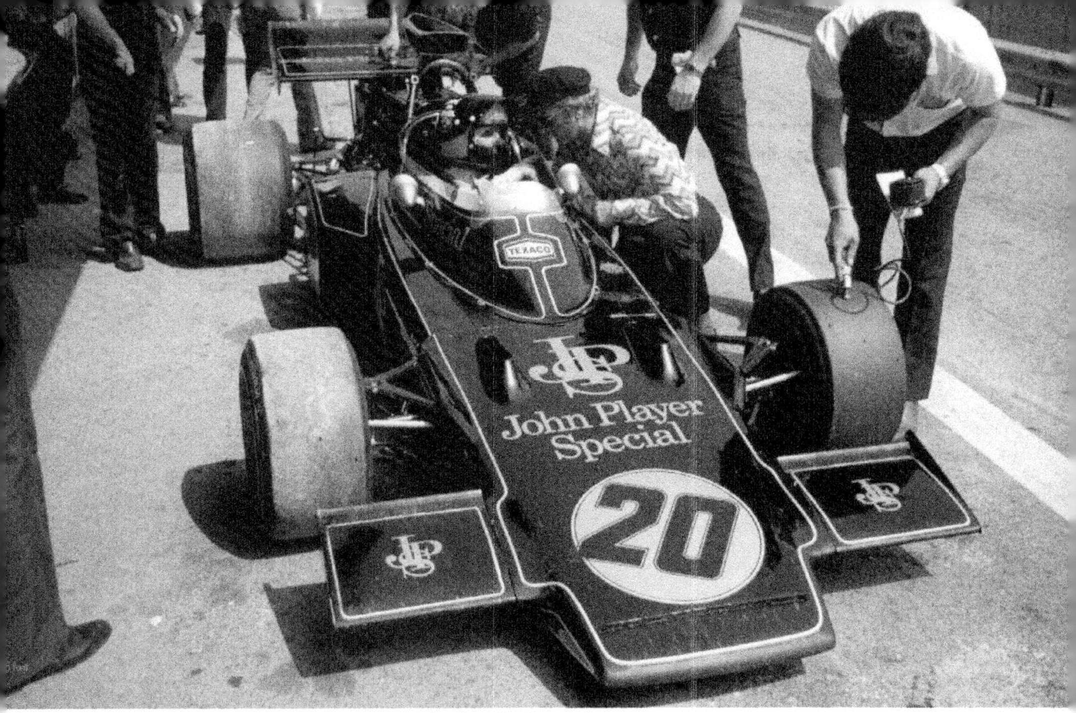

Cochesclasicosdehoy.com

Fitipaldi's meddling and one more from Lotus

In 1972, Stewart would find a great rival who would intrude on his glory: the Brazilian Emerson Fittipaldi. With five victories compared to the four of the British driver, Fittipaldi would be proclaimed champion, also giving the fifth constructors' title to Lotus, demonstrating once again its ability to always be on top.

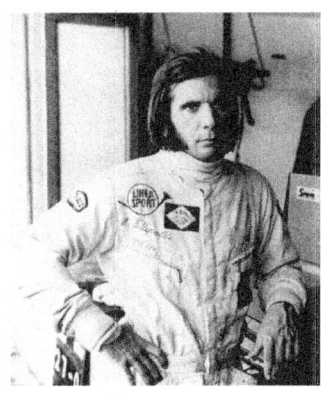

Elcorreo.com

In 1973 the battle between Stewart and Fittipaldi would continue. This time it would be the British who, with six victories compared to the three of the Brazilian, would end up proclaiming himself champion, getting his third title. He would do it one more time aboard a Tyrrell.

However, he could not prevent the constructors' championship from being once again for Lotus, as Fittipaldi would be second in the classification and his partner, the Swede Peterson, third, obtaining the sixth title of Lotus for legend of the team.

Imago-images.de

In 1974, Stewart retired after the death of his partner François Cevert, a fact that affected him emotionally. The British left the competition with three titles achieved. This deprived us of a new fight against Emerson Fittipaldi, who ended up proclaiming himself champion once again, obtaining his second and last world title.

He would get it after his signing for McLaren, who would get his first constructors' title under the name McLaren-Ford. It was not easy to get the final victory, as he achieved it with only three points of advantage over the Swiss Clay Regazzoni, who was driving for a Ferrari team that was missing the victories.

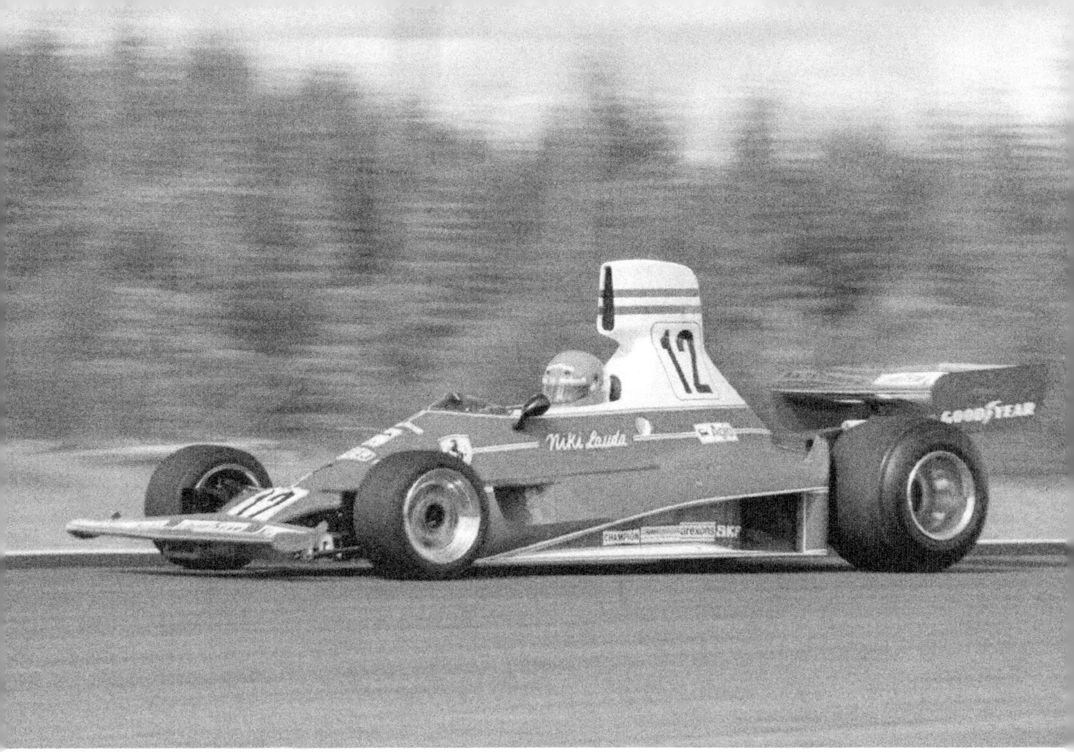

Periodismodelmotor.com

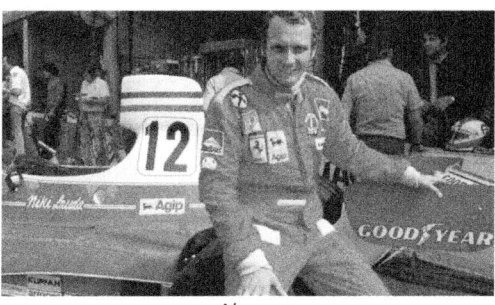

The resurgence of Ferrari

In 1975, Ferrari would manage to rise again to the top. It would not be with the Swiss Regazzoni, who had been runner-up the previous season, but with a historical name in Formula 1: Niki Lauda.

The Austrian led Fittipaldi by almost 20 points to win the drivers 'title and give the Italian team its long-awaited third constructors' title.

Abc.es

The following year, in 1976, Lauda would miss the championship by a single point, and would go to the British James Hunt, who would get his only world title driving for McLaren-Ford.

Automundo.com.ar

Ferrari would at least manage to keep the constructors' title, fourth for the Italian team.

He would not miss his second title in 1977, with a notable advantage over South African driver Jody Scheckter. Ferrari would also be proclaimed champion as a team: fifth title for the Italian team.

F1-fansite.com

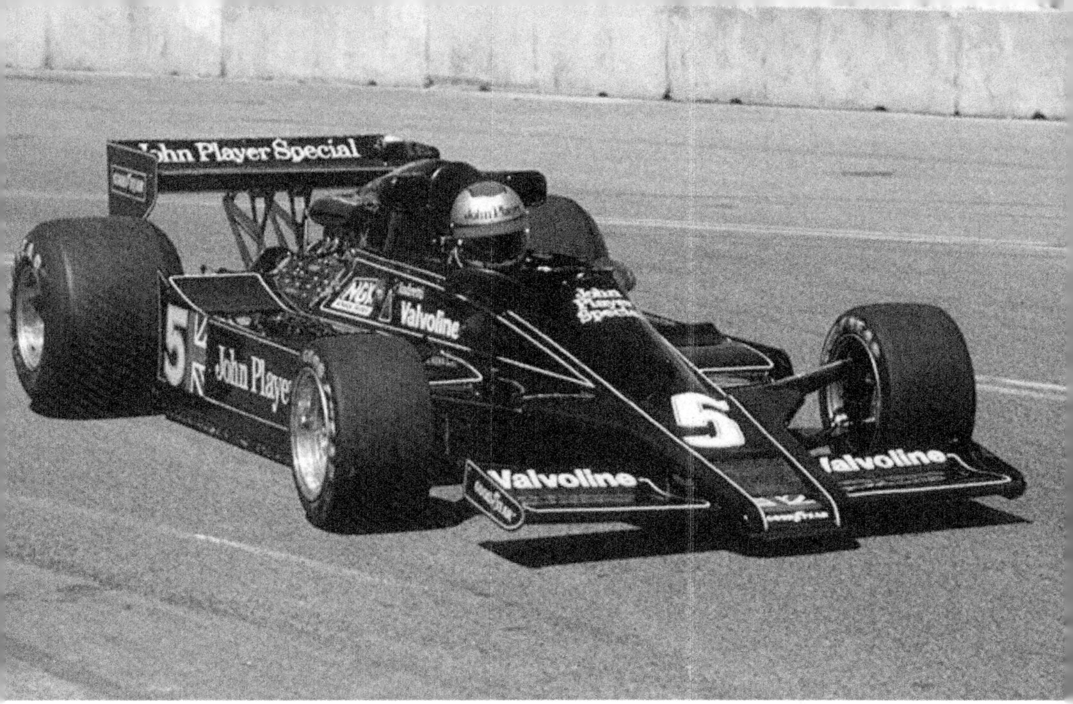

Pinterest.es

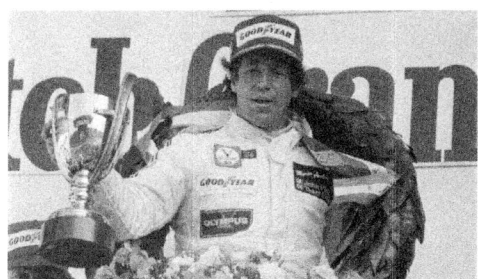

The latest from Lotus and the ground effect

If the history of Formula 1 has shown us anything so far, it is that Lotus had always been there. And if anyone could end the dominance of Lauda and Ferrari, it was the British team. Thus, at the hands of the American Mario Andretti, the team achieved its seventh title, which unfortunately would be the last for the prestigious brand that would have contributed so much to the first years of the competition.

Topgear.es

The success of Lotus was due in large part to the implementation of the "ground effect" in its car for the first time. It is due to an aerodynamic effect of the air that circulates around the car that generates a pressure difference over and under the vehicle in a way that "crushes" it, fixing it to the ground and, above all, allowing higher speeds when cornering.

The new cornering speed coupled with the few means to control it made this effect turn into a deadly effect, so the FIA in 1981 banned the aerodynamic skirts and in 1983 forced the flat bottom that finally ended the practice of the effect ground.

This season, Niki Lauda had chosen to race with Brabham this season, which earned him a total of nine retirements. Despite the fact that the seven grands prix that he did finish did so on the podium, he could not be more than fourth in the final classification.

In 1979, Lotus would deflate. His best position in the final classification would be the seventh position of the Argentine Reutemann, with the champion Andretti descending to twelfth position.

Ferrari would take advantage of it to win its sixth constructors' title, leading South African Jody Scheckter to the top, who would beat his teammate Gilles Villeneuve by four points in an absolute dominance of the Italian team.

Es.wikipedia.org

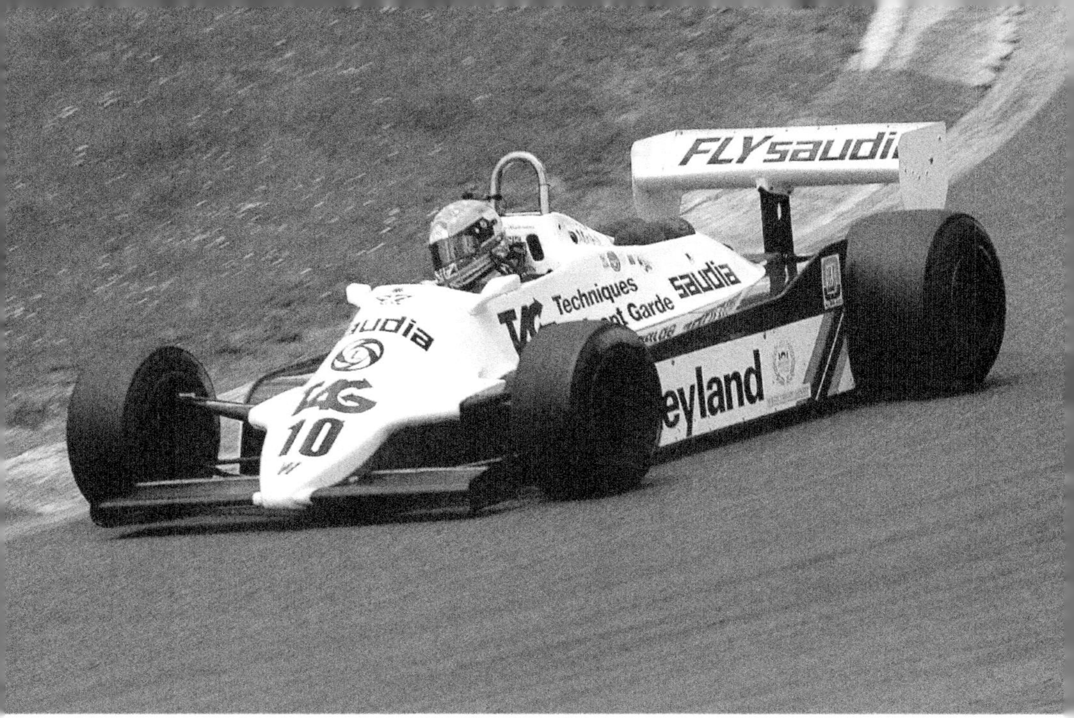

Es.wikipedia.org

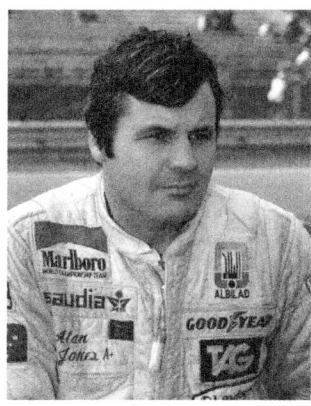

1980: Williams' first

In the 1980 season another of the historic teams entered the scene: Williams. Australian Alan Jones won his first (and only) drivers 'title, in the same way that the Williams-Ford team made its debut in the constructors' title.

Redbull.com

Notable was the disaster at Ferrari, which saw Gilles Villeneuve finish 14th in the final standings in their defense of the title and Scheckter 19th.

In 1981, Williams returned to win the constructors 'title, not being able to get the drivers' title, leaving his pilots Reutemann in second position (just one point behind the title) and Alan Jones third (two points behind the championship).

This highly contested season was won by Brazilian Nelson Piquet driving for Brabham, taking this award-winning driver's first title.

Twitter.com

The following year, in 1982, the opposite would occur. Williams would be able to lead one of his drivers to the world title, but he would not achieve the constructors' title. The lucky one would be the Finn Keke Rosberg, who with a single victory would proclaim himself world champion.

The constructors' championship would be once again for Ferrari, with Frenchman Didier Pironi standing out among its drivers, with Mario Andretti and Gilles Villeneuve dissolving in the final classification.

Ferrari would once again revalidate the title in 1983 thanks to two French drivers: René Arnoux and Patrick Tambay, although the drivers' title would go back to Nelson Piquet, who would achieve his second championship with Brabham.

In this season, the role of Alain Prost stood out, demonstrating the rise of the French drivers, remaining just two points behind the champion with Renault.

Economiahoy.mx

The return of Niki Lauda and the rise of Prost

The alternation between Ferrari, Williams and Piquet was finally overcome by the alliance between McLaren and Porsche. The McLaren-TAG Porsche Turbo team won the constructors' title and brought Austrian Niki Lauda back to glory, who won what would be the last of his championships, third in his career.

This season would be remembered for the battle between Niki Lauda and his partner Alain Prost. The Frenchman was only half a point from the championship, once again being runner-up.

Pinterest.es

After two runners-up, Alain Prost did not want there to be a third and won the title in 1985. He won the championship with a comfortable lead, as his teammate and rival Niki Lauda dropped to the final 10th position. Despite this, McLaren once again revalidated the manufacturers' title.

60years.autosport.com

For his part, Brazilian Ayrton Senna began to appear on the horizon with a fourth position aboard the Lotus.

In 1986, Prost won his second world title, but this time with more difficulties. He only managed to lead Nigel Mansell and his Williams by two points, who had to retire in the last race of the season, although the Frenchman would end up winning it. Behind, Nelson Piquet was three points behind the championship also with Williams-Honda, which would help the team to win the constructors' title. Senna, with Lotus, was fourth again.

In 1987, Prost would be fourth in the standings, giving a break to his rivals, of which Nelson Piquet was the one who got the most out of his Williams to get his third and last world title. Nigel Mansell would return to second and Senna would sneak into third position.

Ayrton Senna, Alain Prost and McLaren

In the recent fight between Williams and McLaren and their alternation in success in recent years, McLaren had not said his last word and snatched the promising Ayrton Senna from Lotus, who claimed his first world title in 1988 and returned to first place to McLaren in the constructors' championship.

McLaren's dominance was overwhelming, managing to win 15 of the 16 races, something that is not surprising, since he had in the squad two great drivers such as Ayrton Senna (who won 8 races) and Alan Prost (who was victorious in 7) . Between them they added more points than the next six teams combined.

Es.wikipedia.org

The Senna-Prost duo continued just as effective in 1989, which was a practical repetition of the previous season, with the exception that this time it was the French who took the title and the Brazilian who was runner-up. The third classified, Ricardo Patrese, was 20 points behind the second classified with a Williams.

Statsf1.com

In this season supercharged engines were banned and it was established that the rider's feet should be behind the front wheels to protect his legs in the event of an accident. The races were limited to 305 kilometers to limit the two hours of duration.

Due to the large number of registrations, a qualifying round was established where only 30 drivers participated in the race. Changes that, seen what has been seen, did not affect the hegemony of McLaren.

In 1990, Alain Prost signed for Ferrari and his place was filled by the Austrian Gerhard Berger. This gave more competitiveness at the constructor level, adding Ferrari to the dispute, although in the individual scenario the battle continued between Prost and Senna, who once again led the rest of their rivals by thirty points.

In this edition, the title returned to the Brazilian's hands and Ayrton Senna surpassed his former teammate Alain Prost. The constructors' title, despite the efforts of Ferrari, which also had Nigel Mansell, continued in the hands of the almighty McLaren-Honda team.

In 1991 final winners were repeated, Ayrton Senna won his third and final drivers 'championship and McLaren-Honda maintained its hegemony with the constructors' championship.

Nigel Mansell, with Williams, was runner-up, a long way behind the Brazilian champion and Alain Prost was fourth with his Ferrari.

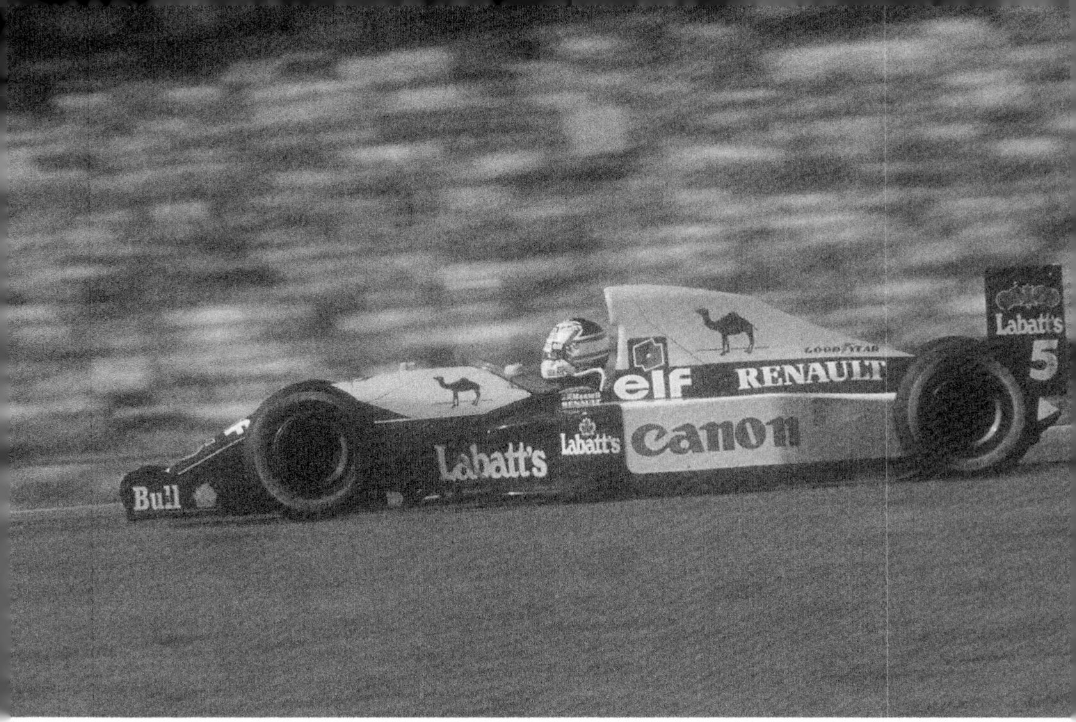

Pinterest.com

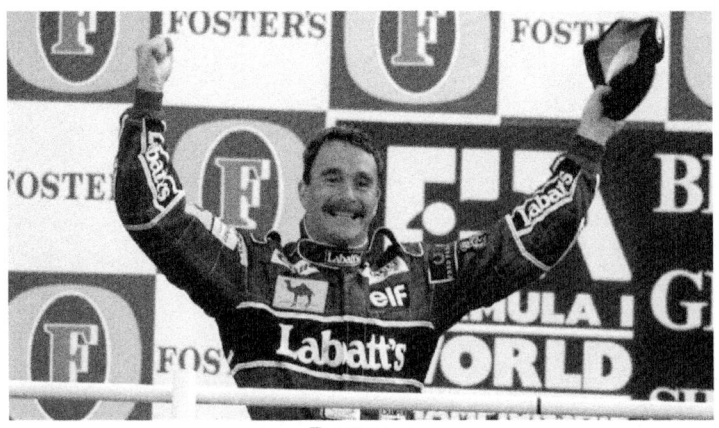

The irruption of Williams

After Mclaren's incessant dominance, Williams became the alternative and in 1992 he managed to prevail by winning the constructors' title and leading Nigel Mansell, finally and after several runners-up, to win the coveted world title.

Topgear.es

Mansell's advantage was considerable, winning 9 grands prix and almost doubling in points the second classified Riccardo Patrese, who was his teammate and who, despite sharing a vehicle, did not get anywhere near his results.

Michael Schumacher's third place stands out this season, aged 23 and driving for Benetton. A prelude to what was to come. Senna was fourth with McLaren in a year that Alain Prost had decided to rest.

Alain Prost would return in 1993, and apparently with a break more than well used, as it served him to return to the top and after signing for Williams-Renault he would get his fourth and last title, before his final retirement.

Pinterest.com.mx

His partner in Williams would be Damon Hill, who would get third place in the final classification, enough for Williams to revalidate the constructors' title. Among them Ayrton Senna would sneak in, with a McLaren that did not give up despite having lost the battle for hegemony. Michael Schumacher continued to add kilometers with Benetton, finishing fourth.

Diariomotor.com

The origin of the Kaiser and Senna's farewell

Michael Schumacher had already been reaping very good results for a team that was not considered among the championship favorites. But what happened in 1994, proclaiming himself champion with 25 years with a Benetton, was a sample of the unlimited talent of the German pilot.

Motorsportnetwork.com

Michael Schumacher came just one point clear of Damon Hill in the final race of the season in Australia. The withdrawal of both in the Australian Grand Prix meant victory in the championship for the German driver.

While a legend began to be forged, another lost his life at the San Marino Grand Prix in Imola. Ayrton Senna's vehicle left straight at the Tamburello curve on lap 7, hitting the concrete wall at 218 km / h. Despite his transfer to the hospital in Bologna, nothing could be done to save his life and he lost a great champion with three world titles and a Formula 1 legend.

Ran.de

In the following season, Michael Schumacher repeated the world title, thus showing that his milestone had not been a matter of luck. In fact, this time he was able to lead his Benetton team to the constructors' championship with the contribution of Johnny Herbert, who finished fourth with less than half the points of the German. Damon Hill was runner-up again, but this time 33 points behind Schumacher. David Coulthard, his teammate at Williams, would clinch third place, but they wouldn't score enough points to overtake Benetton after Schumacher's heroics.

Vice.com

Vice.com

Williams vs. Schumacher-Ferrari

In 1996 Ferrari managed to close the signing of the talented Michael Schumacher, seeking with this extraordinary driver to impose his rhythm in Formula 1 after many years in the shadow of teams such as Williams and McLaren.

It cannot be said that it was a wise decision, since after six retirements (although obtaining three victories), Michael could not achieve more than to reach third place in the final classification.

Damon Hill would not waste this opportunity to stop being in the shadow of the German and would win his first drivers' championship (becoming the first champion son of a champion), twelve points above his partner Jacques Villeneuve, on the record that Williams he kept setting the pace, only interrupted by a Michael Schumacher who had burst in unexpectedly, once again taking the constructors' championship.

Schumacher's teammate at Ferrari, Briton Eddie Irvine, was 10th in the standings with eleven retirements, showing that Michael had not enjoyed a vehicle reliable enough to win the championship. In fact, the drivers of his former Benetton team were fourth (Alesi) and sixth (Bergher), and the question remains whether Schumacher could have beaten the Williams again in his previous team.

In 1997, Williams continued to remain the favorite team, once again winning the constructors 'and drivers' titles, this time going to Canadian Jacques Villeneuve before Hill's march to Arrows.

Villeneuve had to fight a Michael Schumacher who this time did have a more competitive Ferrari and who in fact came in first place in the last race of the championship in Jerez. Michael would try to cause a voluntary collision to prevent the Canadian from overtaking him, although he would finish third in the race proclaiming himself champion, with the German having to retire. For such a performance, the FIA annulled Michael's runner-up.

McLaren returns to the scene

With Williams dominating the scene and Schumacher adapting to a Ferrari capable of contesting a title again, in 1998 one of the great teams enters the scene again: McLaren, with Mercedes engines.

With a hundred points, the Finn Mika Häkkinen won the drivers 'title and, with Coulthard's 56 points (third in the championship), they gave McLaren one more constructors' title.

Pinterest.es

Ferrari became McLaren's greatest rival, with Michael Schumacher finishing second, fourteen points behind the champion and Eddie Irvine fourth. The Williamses, for their part, fell to the third step, but well below the first two teams. Villeneuve was fifth and Frentzen seventh.

In 1999 the battle between McLaren and Ferrari resumed, which would end up sharing titles. Häkkinen would achieve his second consecutive title, but this time it would be the Italian team that would win the constructors' championship.

Twitter.com

Michael Schumacher, who had not finished exploding with Ferrari, is forced to miss six grands prix after the worst accident of his career in Great Britain, so he is replaced by Mika Salo. Despite this, he manages to retain fifth place in the standings, while his teammate Eddie Irvine takes the runner-up, remaining just two points behind Häkkinen. We will never know what Michael could have accomplished if he had not missed six races.

Williams continues to unravel and drops to fifth in the constructors' standings, with Italian Zanardi and Ralf Schumacher (Michael's brother) as drivers. They surprise the good positions of Jordan and Stewart, third and fourth classified.

Pinterest.com

The Schumacher dictatorship

It had to be in 2000, after four unsuccessful seasons with Ferrari, that Michael Schumacher would finally win the world title with the Italian team, something that was bound to happen judging by his talent.

Fukitifu.com

In the panorama the battle between Ferrari and McLaren continued, far above the rest of the teams. Schumacher had to battle with the two McLaren, both Häkkinen and Coulthard, who would finish second and third, battling throughout the championship, although the four consecutive victories in the last grands prix gave Schumacher the coveted title of red.

His teammate, Brazilian Rubens Barrichello, contributed enough points for Ferrari to also win the constructors' title.

Lafm.com.co

Williams, who had signed Britain's Jenson Button, climbed to third place this season, partially recovering, although still far behind Ferrari and McLaren.

In 2001 the trend not only continued along the same lines, but Ferrari's dominance became more accentuated. Schumacher would manage to win nine races (none of his partner Barrichello), compared to two for Coulthard. This meant that Michael nearly doubled the second-placed Briton in points and Ferrari added 179 points to Mclaren's 102, opening a gap between them. Meanwhile, Williams closed the gap to McLaren in third place.

Diariomotor.com

In 2002, the Ferrari-Schumacher dominance would be tougher if possible. Schumacher would double in points to his partner Barrichello, second classified, and in turn the Italian team would double the score to the second classified team, which would become Williams, which in addition to Ralf Schumacher, had the Colombian Juan Pablo Montoya.

Youtube.com

For its part, McLaren accused the withdrawal of Häkkinen and despite having a talented Kimi Räikkönen alongside Coulthard, the team fell to third place losing a large number of points.

In 2003, the scoring positions were extended to eight, with no limit on scoring races, but this change did not affect a Michael Schumacher who once again won the world title, fourth in a row with Ferrari and sixth personal. Despite the fact that the Italian team would win back the constructors' title, it did not show the authority of previous years, showing first signs of weakness.

This was demonstrated in the disputed drivers' title, in which Kimi Räikkönen with McLaren still had options in the final race in Japan and would ultimately be just two points behind the German six-time champion.

Matraxlubricantes.com

The differences between constructors also became smaller. Ferrari was only 14 points ahead of Williams, second classified, and they only got two points more than the third: McLaren. This opened a championship that was no longer dominated by Ferrari, but was a matter of three. Behind, all the teams stayed quite far, although Renault closed with 88 points a very good season.

In 2004, Formula 1 expanded in Asia with the inclusion of the Bahrain and Chinese Grand Prix, thus expanding its market in a sample of the great racing business, accentuated above all by the figure of Bernie Ecclestone, who since the In the 1970s, in which the British magnate obtained the sale of television rights, he had always had financial control of the competition and guarded his ability to generate money, until in 2017 he was replaced by the Liberty Media company.

But focusing on the sports plane, 2004 was the year in which Schumacher closed a wonderful cycle with Ferrari, achieving the fifth consecutive title for the team, and the seventh in the German personal account, a record so far unbeaten.

While the previous season seemed to have evened out between teams, at least among the top three, Ferrari re-dominated as it had been doing years ago, beating second-ranked by 143 points.

Within the team, things would not change much. Schumacher would be the undisputed leader with an impressive 13 races won. In Monaco he had to retire, and finished on the podium in Belgium and Italy. His twelfth place in China and seventh in Brazil closed a spectacular year.

For his part, Rubens Barrichello, had to settle once again with being his squire, always in the shadow of the German, and finished in second place, 32 points behind the kaiser.

Thebestf1.es

Although Ferrari's dominance remained as in the previous five years, the surprise this season came for the rest of the teams. Williams dropped to fourth place and McLaren dropped to fifth place. What unexpected teams slipped over these two legends taking their places?

The third classified would be Renault (which had already ceased to be Benetton since 2001), a half surprise since the previous season it had already been doing things quite well. This success was due in large part to a young Alonso, who at the age of 23 achieved fourth place in the standings, getting four podiums and always finishing in the top seven except for the five grands prix that he had to retire.

The previous season he had already achieved his first victory and achieved three podiums with Renault in Hungary, after signing for the French team (the previous year he had debuted in Formula 1 with Minardi), thus showing his talent. In 2003 he had finished sixth in the standings, and a great future loomed for him.

His teammate Jarno Trulli finished sixth to add 46 points for the good season for Mild Seven Renault.

Es.wikipedia.org

The other team that surprised in the 2004 season was the BAR-Honda team, which included Jenson Button (third place in the world championship) and the Japanese Takuma Sato (eighth).

Twitter.com

Alonso and the end of the Ferrari-Schumacher era

After five years of absolute domination of Ferrari thanks to Michael Schumacher, it was difficult to think that his reign could be ended easily, or at least in the short term. In this scenario, in 2005 Fernando Alonso and Renault emerged to end the dynasty of the Italian team. Paradoxes of fate, Schumacher saw his streak of five consecutive World Cups broken by the mark that gave him his first World Cup.

This season there were several regulatory changes that could have affected the end of Ferrari's reign. The most significant rule was the fact that it was no longer possible to change tires at the pit stops (except for a puncture or the appearance of rain). The engines in turn had to be used in two consecutive grands prix, instead of one per race. Important aerodynamic changes were also made to the wings to take advantage of the slipstream and make overtaking easier.

Whether due to the changes or not, Michael Schumacher finished third in the final classification, being surpassed in addition to by the champion Alonso, by Kimi Räikkönen, who was driving for McLaren. Ferrari's performance decline was evident with Barrichello's eighth position, so Schumacher probably squeezed the best out of the car, clinching a single victory in the United States.

As for the rest of the teams, McLaren regained positions and between Räikkönen and Juan Pablo Montoya (who had to be replaced by Pedro de la Rosa and Wurz in two races) they contested the title with Renault until the last race.

Ferrari was well below both teams (Renault almost doubled them in points), and in fact their fight was with another of the teams in an unexpected result: Toyota. Williams, fifth, seemed unable to find himself again and BAR-Honda dropped to sixth.

In 2006, Alonso and Renault revalidated their titles, continuing their good understanding of the previous season. The fight to get the title was also very close this time. However, the competition would be against Ferrari, which seemed to be recovering from its bad previous year and had brought in Massa to replace Barrichello. In turn, it was Fisichella who was replacing Trulli at Renault.

Motorist.com

McLaren regained third place with Räikkönen and Juan Pablo Montoya (in the first half of the championship) and De la Rosa (second half of the championship) among their ranks. The fourth place was this time also for a Japanese team, in this case Honda.

This year, tire changes had also returned, and the engines had been downgraded to 2.4L V8s instead of 3L V10s.

2007: The return of Ferrari

Ferrari had already warned Renault the previous season that it wanted to regain its throne in Formula 1 and made good on its threat in the 2007 season. This year the evolution of V8 engines was frozen for ten seasons to save costs.

However, it was not Michael Schumacher who would bring glory back to the Italian team, as the previous season he had announced his retirement to become a Ferrari driver advisor. His place would be taken by the Finnish Kimi Räikkönen, the "ice man."

The end of the season would be hotly contested, with three drivers fighting for the title in the last Brazilian Grand Prix. One of them was the two-time champion Fernando Alonso, who had signed for McLaren in 2007, thus ending his five-year cycle with Renault.

The other driver involved would be a very young 22-year-old Lewis Hamilton, who shared a team with Alonso at McLaren and who made his debut in Formula 1. The British would get second place in the championship with four victories, equaling in triumphs and points to his partner Fernando Alonso. Both would be just one point behind the Finnish champion.

Giantbomb.com

Although between Alonso and Hamilton they added enough points to win the constructors' world title, the McLaren team was sanctioned for spying on Ferrari, canceling all the points obtained in the season and relegating the team to last place. The title would therefore remain for the Italian team by adding Massa's points to those achieved by the champion.

Motor.es

Although the fight for the title was reduced to two teams, Ferrari and McLaren, it is worth highlighting the role of the BMW Sauber team, second classified after the elimination of McLaren, and that Heidfeld and Kubica would get more than a hundred points. In the United States, Kubica's BMW would be driven by Vettel, who by then was already racing with Toro Rosso.

Es.wikipedia.org

Carpixel.net

The origin of a new super champion

In 2008 Formula 1 was about to suffer a strong split (with the possible creation of a parallel championship) due to the difficulty of many of its teams to survive economically. The conflict was settled with the Agreement of Concord that improved the conditions regarding the distribution of income for many of them. This year, the controversial qualification system based on three rounds is also established: Q1, Q2 and Q3.

In the previous season, with Lewis Hamilton falling just one point behind the champion on his debut, it had become clear that a new champion was in the making and that sooner or later he would win a world title. What nobody could have expected is that it would be so soon, since in 2007 and with a stroke of justice, he managed to win the championship by a single point against Felipe Massa's Ferrari.

Lat.motorsport.com

However, the stratospheric talent of Lewis Hamilton was not enough for McLaren to win the constructors' title, as his teammate Heikki Kovalainen could not get past seventh. Alonso had left the team to return to Renault, finishing fifth in the final classification.

The teams title would be again for Ferrari, with Massa second and Räikkönen third and a 21-point lead over silver bullets.

Pinterest.com

BMW, with Heidfeld and Kubica, continued its good work, once again becoming the first team in the rest of the classification and getting dangerously close to McLaren. This showed that in the BMW-Williams spin-off, the German team had fared better, as Williams lagged far behind their best times in eighth.

Es.wikipedia.org

Youtube.com

The irruption of Brawn GP

In 2009, in the middle of a fight between Ferrari and McLaren-Mercedes, a new team appeared that was going to break all the rules of Formula 1: Brawn GP.

In this season the KERS appeared, an Energy Recovery System that takes advantage of part of the energy dissipated in the form of heat by the brakes to transform it into electrical energy and give an extra power to the motors for a few seconds before discharging. In turn, the engines were forced to be used for three races.

This season, the Japanese teams Toyota and Honda, due to their poor sporting and economic results, were about to withdraw from the championship. In fact, Toyota would do it at the end of the year with BMW.

However, Honda underwent a makeover, becoming a new team: Brawn GP. And this change would not be merely testimonial at all.

With Mercedes engines and Jenson Button and Rubens Barrichello at the helm, Brawn won the constructors 'title, as well as the drivers' title for the British, showing a superiority not without suspicion. In fact, except for China, the team won six of the first seven races, largely thanks to blower exhausts to take advantage of the ground effect that was very close to the regulations due to its size.

These exhausts were also used in Toyota, as if they wanted to give some additional help to the teams that were suffering the most economic problems. When the rest of the teams developed their exhausts around the Brawn model, the results ended up being equal, but by then the British team had already reaped a lot of points.

Pinterest.co.kr

Among the superiority shown by Brawn-Mercedes was a 22-year-old Sebastian Vettel, already promoted to the Red Bull first team, a team that proved to be the most competitive of the rest of the grid, with Australian Mark Webber finishing fourth. This would be a meteoric and unexpected rise for the energy drinks team, the only one capable of standing up to Brawn, finally being less than 20 points.

Zimbio.com

Hamilton and Kovalainen's McLaren took third place in the standings, with a rather poor performance that the Briton managed to squeeze for two victories, although his Finnish teammate would finish twelfth in the final standings. Ferrari, which had to use up to four drivers (Massa, Badoer, Fisichella and Räikkönen) fell one point behind McLaren.

The era of Vettel and Red Bull

After the controversial Brawn GP season, his rider Mercedes bought more than 75% of the team and the German team returned as such to Formula 1 after many years of absence.

It would not be the only sounded comeback, since with the German team itself the seven-time champion Michael Schumacher would return to racing, which was quite a mystery to see if he would be able to return with the same performance as in his years of triumph.

Also Sauber returned to the competition replacing BMW and the once successful Lotus also returned. The world champion, Jenson Button, after the disappearance of Brawn, would join the McLaren Mercedes team with Lewis Hamilton.

Thus, with so much change, there were many unknowns on the asphalt that Sebastian Vettel quickly began to clear up, continuing with his progress and good work the previous season, and who would end up getting his first world title and the first also for the Red brand Bull (with Renault engines) as a construction company. Vettel broke the youth record for a world title at 23 years and 4 months, set shortly before by Lewis Hamilton (23 years and 9 months).

Redbull.com

Vettel would become a very tight champion, since he was only 4 points ahead of the second classified, Fernando Alonso, who this season was competing with Ferrari.

Momentogp.com

Australian Mark Webber took third place in the standings, showing the good work of the Red Bull team and Lewis Hamilton would be relegated to fourth place. With Button fifth place, the McLaren team was Red Bull's main competitor, as Felipe Massa's sixth place made Ferrari have to settle for third place.

Fourth would be the brand new Mercedes team on a satisfactory start, but far from the top three and with results far removed from their previous line-up as Brawn. Renault, for its part, achieved an acceptable fifth place after having remained in the competition for very little citing financial problems.

The return of the kaiser with Mercedes was not what is said to be very successful, finishing in seventh position and with practically half the points of his teammate Nico Rosberg.

Tudn.com

The following season would repeat champions, Vettel and Red Bull getting the second consecutive title, opening a new era, just as it was happening in Formula 1 in recent times with teams dominating through stages.

This, despite the introduction of one of the most decisive changes in recent times, the DRS system: a mobile spoiler that takes advantage of the slipstream of the car in front when it is less than a second away, providing an advantage that facilitates overtaking. .

This time the German won with much more calm and advantage (with 122 points over Jenson Button's McLaren), demonstrating that Vettel's talent was gaining in maturity, making him an unbeatable driver.

Maxf1.net

The third classified was again the other Red Bull of Mark Webber and Fernando Alonso could only be fourth with Ferrari. Behind him was Lewis Hamilton.

In the constructors' championship, this translated into Red Bull dominance, with McLaren second, well above the rest, but unable to compete against the Austrian energy drink team.

Third, also in no man's land, would be the Ferrari of Alonso and Massa. The fourth place again would be for Mercedes (with Schumacher as eighth classified) and in the fifth position would be Renault this time as Lotus-Renault.

In 2012, despite having the exceptionality of 6 champion drivers on the grid (Vettel, Alonso, Schumacher, Hamilton, Button and Räikkönen), the results would not be very different either. Vettel would manage with Red Bull to keep the drivers and constructors title, third for both.

Automobilsport.com

However, the advantage this time would be reduced and Vettel would have to suffer for his third consecutive title. Not all was decided until the last race in Brazil, as Alonso had options with Ferrari, although like two years earlier, the Spaniard would have to settle for finishing second in the standings.

Tusruedas.wordpress.com

Surprising third place for Kimi Räikkönen in the Lotus-Renault. Hamilton and Button would occupy the next places in the final classification and Michael Schumacher, 13th and well below his teammate Rosberg in Mercedes, would finally decide to retire definitively thus ending his career in Formula 1. Without having been able to regain glory in the German team Thus, the seven-time world champion retired.

Tn.com.ar

Regarding the constructors' title, there was greater equality between Red Bull, Ferrari (2nd classified) and McLaren. Even Renault achieved a good result accumulating more than 300 points. Mercedes this time would be fifth, below the French team.

Did this new equality and rapprochement mean that the Red Bull era was over? Well, the truth is that, in 2013, the last season of V8 engines, Vettel and Red Bull once again won the two world titles, the fourth in a row for driver and manufacturer.

In fact, far from the results contracting further, Vettel achieved his fourth title with an advantage of more than 150 points over Alonso, who, once again, was runner-up and in the shadow of Red Bull and the German driver.

The most striking change throughout the Red Bull era was the rise of Mercedes this season, which, while unable to compete against the Austrian team, would still manage to reach second place in the standings six points ahead of Ferrari.

In this would have a lot to do, in addition to the poor performance of Massa (the other Ferrari driver), the signing of Mercedes by Lewis Hamilton to replace the recently retired Michael Schumacher. Hamilton, in fourth place, would get 189 points thus showing what would be the prelude to a successful alliance with the German team.

Curvasenlazadas.com

Also striking would be the disaster for McLaren, which after the loss of Lewis and with Button and Sergio Pérez at the helm, would drop to fifth place below the Renault team (from Räikkönen and Grosjean, with Kovalainen participating in the last two races).

The reign of Mercedes and the records of Hamilton

In 2014, in addition to a new Concord Agreement between the Builders Association and the FIA that gave more prominence to the teams in the negotiation of television rights, 1,600 cc turbo engines and 8 gearboxes were introduced. gears, so the best-suited team would start with a big advantage.

That team was undoubtedly Mercedes, which continued its progress from the previous season to once again reign as a team in Formula 1. It would do so thanks to Lewis Hamilton, a driver who was undoubtedly key in the revival of the brand and who obtained his second world title.

Key would also be the new power units with energy recovery system in braking and exhaust that would mark the future of Mercedes as the best motorcyclist of the hybrid and Formula 1 era.

Bolsamania.com

Mercedes' dominance was overwhelming, with 701 points to Red Bull's 405, which saw its dominance end with the Mercedes almost insultingly outscoring everyone, winning 16 of the 19 races. In fact, Hamilton was first in the standings and his teammate Rosberg, second, a long way from third: Mark Webber's Red Bull.

The Williamses, thanks to the Mercedes engines, achieved third place in the constructors' classification with the pilots Felipe Massa and the Finn Valtteri Bottas, in what they pointed to as a recovery of this legendary team that had had too many years of poor results.

M.F1network.net

The one that would go on a downward trajectory would be another of the greats, McLaren, which would finish in fifth place. Ferrari did not have a great adaptation to the new power units either, finishing fourth, with Alonso sixth and Räikkönen 13th. Both teams are far from Williams, Red Bull, and what to say about Mercedes.

After these convulsive changes, in 2015 it was expected that the teams would have adapted better to the hybrid era. The Virtual Safety Car was also established, in which in case of a minor accident or in which there was no imminent danger, instead of leaving the Safety Car regrouping the cars, a speed limitation was established until the danger passed, maintaining distances .

In any case, the dominance of Mercedes was brutal again (again 16 of 19 victories). The team repeated the championship and Lewis Hamilton took his third world title.

Motor1.com

The dominance of the German team was again excessive, with 703 points compared to the 428 of the second classified, which in this case was Ferrari again after the inclusion of four-time champion Sebastian Vettel as Räikkönen's teammate (Alonso became part of the team McLaren).

Hamilton and Rosberg reigned supreme in the drivers' standings, followed by the two Ferrari drivers. Fifth and sixth would be the two Williams drivers: Bottas and Massa, respectively. The British team continued its recovery and aimed to return to better times.

Autosport.com

Red Bull was in fourth position (with Ricciardo and Kvyat), and those times when it dominated the scene seemed long ago. McLaren was in fifth position after abandoning Mercedes engines and joining forces with Honda.

2016 would be another year of dominance by Mercedes Petronas (19 of 21 races), although that season Lewis Hamilton would give a breather to the drivers' title and would be surpassed by his teammate, the German Nico Rosberg. Only 5 points separated the two drivers and the championship was close to the end, but the fact of dominating the scene and not having more drivers between them made them finish first and second in the last race, with a title for Rosberg.

Motor.ru

As for the rest of the teams, they were still in the background of the Formula 1 scene. Red Bull regained at least second place in the constructors' championship, and it did so with the emergence of a talented Max Verstappen, who, if Well he was behind his partner Ricciardo, he was already pointing ways to become the youngest driver to win a race at the Spanish Grand Prix (18 years, 7 months and 15 days).

Motor1.com

Third was the Ferrari team, a relative distance from Red Bull, and far behind were the Force India and Williams teams, both with Mercedes engines. The alliance between McLaren and Honda did not bear fruit, and the British team remained in sixth position.

In 2017, champion Nico Rosberg was retiring citing excessive competitive pressure and his position at Mercedes was held by Valtteri Bottas. The Finn, despite his good work, was not competitive enough to face Lewis Hamilton who won his fourth world title, third in a row for the Mercedes team that, once again, easily surpassed its rivals, although Ferrari he was able to put up a certain battle with Vettel and Räikkönen, reducing Mercedes' victories to 12 compared to five for the Italian team.

Gossipvehiculo.com

Red Bull was third again, far behind Ferrari and its pursuers, with a Max Verstappen ever closer to Ricciardo.

Force India, with the Mexican Sergio Pérez and the French Esteban Ocon, would be the fourth team maintaining the good work of the Indian team.

As for the historical teams, Williams would have to settle for fifth place and McLaren would begin to suffer from the poor decision to feed on Honda engines by descending to ninth place, the penultimate team that was only able to surpass Sauber in a season disaster.

2018 would not be much different, keeping the battle between Mercedes and Ferrari, still with notable superiority of the German team (11 victories against six). The individual fight would be between Hamilton and Vettel, with victory for the British adding his fifth personal title.

It should be noted that, due to the superiority of Mercedes, if anyone could bring excitement to the championship, it was his teammate Bottas, who did not achieve any victory all season.

Essentiallysports.com

In this two-color fight (if it can be called a fight), Max Verstappen became the best of Red Bull beating Ricciardo and positioning himself above Bottas, sneaking between the Ferraris and Mercedes.

Therefore, Mercedes, Ferrari and Red Bull would be the first three classified in the constructors' world championship as the previous season. The surprises would come below. Renault would finish in fourth place, followed by Haas, an American team that had joined in 2016 and whose vehicle had been considered a copy of Ferrari.

F1experiences.com

McLaren continued its ordeal, although now with Renault engines it would at least manage to regain sixth place and move away from the final positions. The drama would come this time for Williams, who would only manage to avoid the last position with the exclusion of Force India, which would end up reappearing the following season as Racing Point with the purchase of the team by Lawrence Stroll, father of the pilot Lance Stroll.

2019 would be one more season of sum and it continues for Mercedes, with 15 victories. Only three victories for Max Verstappen for Red Bull and three for Ferrari, one for Vettel and two for Charles Leclerc, escaped him.

Regarding the internal world of Mercedes, although Bottas achieved four victories, he was far from Hamilton's eleven, in what seems to be a comfortable companion for the Briton and also for the team that avoids major competitiveness conflicts.

It is not such a good thing for the viewer. At a stage where only one Mercedes can compete against another Mercedes, we are deprived of at least one more close fight between its two drivers.

Essentiallysports.com

Special mention the debut in Formula 1 of Leclerc, a pilot called to achieve great things. Not only because of his record of being the youngest driver to win two consecutive races (at 21 years, 10 months and 22 days), but also because of his character and his driving ability, surpassing a four-time champion like Sebastian Vettel in his first season. increasingly worn out by Ferrari's inability to stand up to Mercedes. Leclerc has become the hope for the future of a possible revival of the Italian team.

Autobild.es

In 2019, Mercedes once again achieved a comfortable victory, with a Ferrari in second place looking more in the rearview mirror trying to retain its second place against Red Bull than trying to overtake the all-powerful German team.

In fact, Max Verstappen was the first classified driver behind the two Mercedes, in a more mature degree than this Dutch driver who has talent to spare to mark an era. Such is his quality that Red Bull is unable to find a partner to match, demoting Pierre Gasly to his secondary team Toro Rosso this season and moving from him to Thai Alexander Albon.

Actualidadmotor.com

As for the rest of the teams, 2019 arrives as a light breeze of fresh air for McLaren, which achieves the fourth position, becoming the first team of the so-called "second division", with talented Carlos Sainz Jr. and Lando Norris squeezing the maximum the vehicle of the British team. Renault continues in an uncertain fifth place, with the constant threat of leaving the competition for economic reasons. And Williams continues with his drama, not only by falling to the last position in the classification, but by doing so without having competitive capacity, always last in the classification and doubled in practically every race. A legendary team ... in its worst days.

2020 and... the future?

2020 was called to be another year of transition without major changes. Aware of the monotony and boredom that the superiority of Mercedes has been causing in the spectator for several years, depriving them of emotion and considering each race as a repetition of the previous one with the German team rising (almost) always with the victory, for 2021 he had established a revolutionary regulation.

This regulation, under the pretext of adjusting budgets to lower costs, is called to balance teams due to the economic limits, to equalize them in monetary levels so that this ends up translating into equality on the track. Formula 1 knows how important it is to retain the fan, especially in these times of such diversity of entertainment pay television. And that requires more equality in the races and less predictability and monotony.

However, the coronavirus pandemic broke out disrupting all the plans of Formula 1, as well as of sports in general. With the championship and the development of the vehicles paralyzed, the new regulation was delayed (at least) until 2022.

This means that the Formula 1 revolution will have to wait another year and that, not only that, but 2020 and 2021 are expected to be a copy of what we are already seeing on the track. The teams prefer to invest in the new regulation, and not in a regulation that is set to expire, in addition to the limitation of tokens for new evolutions in order to reduce expenses.

However, it was to be expected that this 2020 the only thing that would change in the Mercedes was its color (with its black coloration in protest of the anti-racist movement Blacks lives matter). In fact, in the thirteenth race and with four remaining to finish the championship, Mercedes won the constructors' championship at Imola, the seventh in a row since 2014.

Diariomotor.com

One of the remaining unknowns was whether Lewis Hamilton would achieve his seventh world title, thus equaling seven-time champion Michael Schumacher as the two drivers to win the most world titles. Bottas did not put up much resistance as in previous years and Lewis Hamilton was proclaimed driver's champion in Turkey, a race after his team did. The Briton makes history with his seven titles and thus equals the kaiser's championship record.

Mundodeportivo.com

At the top, the question is whether Ferrari will be able to compete face to face against Mercedes once and for all. Or rather, it was. The first races have been devastating for the Italian team, with very poor results, one of the worst seen in a long time at Ferrari, with a vehicle with a very limited speed, with a performance well below Mercedes, even with difficulties to stay in the part average of the ranking.

Ferrari's start in 2020 is very, very sad. The poor performance of the car further deepens the frustration of Vettel, who after the disputes with the management and knowing himself outside the team, thinks more about his future than about his present.

Leclerc, for his part, has shown his talent in the first part of the 2020 season, beating his teammate, the four-time champion Vettel in results.

Autobild.es

Faced with the collapse of Ferrari, the alternative to Mercedes has only one name: Max Verstappen. The Dutchman, who has extended his commitment to Red Bull, is the only one capable of showing some competence. The results of his partner Alex Albon are rather scarce. We will have to see Max in a more even Formula 1, increasingly focused and less impetuous, since he has the talent to become a champion of the time.

Revistasafetycar.com

McLaren, for its part, will try to be the first of the so-called "second division", a division that this 2020 has started very tight. Behind the Mercedes (and Verstappen), equality is maximum. If the German team were removed, we would be facing one of the most contested championships in recent times. Carlos Sainz (already with the signing with Ferrari to replace Vettel in 2021) and Lando Norris will try to follow the upward trajectory of a McLaren that, far from its best times, seems to recover little by little.

Motor.es

Renault has, despite its internal difficulties, competing against McLaren for several years in that fight to be the first of the rest. Although the British seem to be winning over the French, Renault must have no other aspiration than to continue competing with them. For this they have the good work of Ricciardo since his arrival, and with the return of Esteban Ocon.

Diariomotor.com

The Racing Point thing is another story. Accustomed to the half table, to scoring comfortably, and to being a competitive team, no one was expecting this year's quality jump. He was not expected so high, reaching the third place in terms of team performance. However, their improvement has not been without suspicion, accused of copying last year's Mercedes, which has led to the nickname of the "pink Mercedes". Despite the financial sanction and fifteen points, they will be able to continue using their improvements based on the Mercedes (especially their brakes), so it will be a team to take into account throughout 2020, whose performance will depend on know-how of the Mexican Sergio Pérez (who missed two races for testing positive for coronavirus) and Lance Stroll.

Formularapida.net

From the Toro Rosso team, renamed AlphaTauri, the usual is expected. Make it competitive ... and no. The Red Bull affiliate team has been seen over time both comfortable in the points positions, and close to the last classified, with variations even within the same season. It remains to be seen if the change of name (and color) makes them break this oscillatory trend. We will also have to look at the performance of Pierre Gasly and whether he will be able to regain his seat at Red Bull, snatched by Alexander Albon. So far, Gasly has achieved victory in Italy in a very competitive AlphaTauri.

Viajesycarreras.com

As for the Alfa Romeos, who even fought for points last season when the weekend was right for them, they have seen a deterioration in their performance that has taken them to the last positions. A tough year is expected for the Swiss team fighting in the queue.

Formula1.lne.es

Another team that has seen its performance diminish is the North American Haas, largely because of its Ferrari engine. The team, which in its best days has had no difficulty to position itself in the middle table, this year fights against Alfa Romeo and Williams for not occupying the last positions. Curious about this team, which once again supports Grosjean and Magnussen, when they have proven to be two drivers with some irregularity.

Fast-mag.com

And finally, it remains the question of whether the collapse of Williams becomes definitive, with the consequent sadness of seeing a legend of Formula 1 in his position. For now, the team has had to be bought by the investment firm Dorilton Capital, with no choice but to resort to this sale to continue surviving. This year it seems to be slightly higher than the previous one (which was hard to get worse), and George Russell is at least able to compete with some rivals at the rear, while rookie Latifi racks up his first kilometers. We will have to see the drift of this historical team, which does not predict a great future.

Soymotor.com

We'll see what 2020 has in store for us, with an eye on whether Hamilton will take advantage of this season and the next to overtake Schumacher and become the only driver with eight titles, before the true Formula 1 revolution arrives in 2022.

ANNEXED
Drivers with the most titles

Pilot	Titles	Years
Michael Schumacher	7	1994, 1995, 2000, 2001, 2002, 2003, 2004
Lewis Hamilton	7	2008, 2014, 2015, 2017, 2018, 2019, 2020
Juan Manuel Fangio	5	1951, 1954, 1955, 1956, 1957
Sebastian Vettel	4	2010, 2011, 2012, 2013
Alain Prost	4	1985, 1986, 1989, 1993
Jack Brabham	3	1959, 1960, 1966
Jackie Stewart	3	1969, 1971, 1973
Niki Lauda	3	1975, 1977, 1984
Nelson Piquet	3	1981, 1983, 1987
Ayrton senna	3	1988, 1990, 1991
Alberto ascari	2	1952, 1953
Jim Clark	2	1963, 1965
Graham hill	2	1962, 1968
Emerson Fittipaldi	2	1972, 1974
Mika Hakkinen	2	1998, 1999
Fernando Alonso	2	2005, 2006
Giuseppe Farina	1	1950

Mike Hawthorn	**1**	1958
Phil Hill	**1**	1961
John Surtees	**1**	1964
Denny Hulme	**1**	1967
Jochen rindt	**1**	1970
James hunt	**1**	1976
Mario andretti	**1**	1978
Jody scheckter	**1**	1979
Alan Jones	**1**	1980
Keke rosberg	**1**	1982
Nigel Mansell	**1**	1992
Damon Hill	**1**	1996
Jacques villeneuve	**1**	1997
Kimi raikkonen	**1**	2007
Jenson button	**1**	2009
Nico Rosberg	**1**	2016

ANNEXED
Builders with more titles

Builder	Titles	Years
Ferrari	16	1961, 1964, 1975, 1976, 1977, 1979, 1982, 1983, 1999, 2000, 2001, 2002, 2003, 2004, 2007, 2008
Williams	9	1980, 1981, 1986, 1987, 1992, 1993, 1994, 1996, 1997
Mclaren	8	1974, 1984, 1985, 1988, 1989, 1990, 1991, 1998
Mercedes	7	2014, 2015, 2016, 2017, 2018, 2019, 2020
Lotus	7	1963, 1965, 1968, 1970, 1972, 1973, 1978
Red bull	4	2010, 2011, 2012, 2013
Cooper	2	1959, 1960
Brabham	2	1966, 1967
Renault	2	2005, 2006
Vanwall	1	1958
Benetton	1	nineteen ninety five
BRM	1	1962
Matra	1	1969
Tyrrell	1	1971
Brawn	1	2009

THANKS

To all of you who encourage my love of motorsport, which has been the germ of this work.

To all of you who enjoy Formula 1 and make this a shared passion.

To all those who have made a note or correction (and that you will continue to do) to create a more truthful and accurate title.

To all the graphic resources referred to, for making this text attractive.

To all of you who send me your opinions and make this book something collective.

Many thanks.
Charles Sanz.

Printed in Great Britain
by Amazon